KANSAS CITY

Kansas City

A collection of short stories
by

CHRISTOPHER ASLAN OVERFELT

BOOKS

Adelaide Books
New York / Lisbon
2020

KANSAS CITY
A collection of short stories
By Christopher Aslan Overfelt

Published by Adelaide Books, New York / Lisbon
adelaidebooks.org

Editor-in-Chief
Stevan V. Nikolic

For any information, please address Adelaide Books
at info@adelaidebooks.org

or write to:

Adelaide Books
244 Fifth Ave. Suite D27
New York, NY, 10001

ISBN: 978-1-952570-92-6

Printed in the United States of America

Contents

Intro Speculum

Prospero's Books sits on the NW corner of 39th and Ball street, in Kansas City. It sits next to a sushi joint in a two story brick building, the ground level of which has two windowed walls, facing east and southward. Outside the windows, on the sidewalk, are a few wooden tables with stacks of books selling at a discount price. It is here that Pyramus pauses and peruses, being the cheap guy that he is, always on the lookout for a deal. His girlfriend, Thisbe, scans the titles as well, and then he follows her into the bookstore.

They have just enjoyed a sushi dinner, and are out for an evening walk, Pyramus burping up a mixture of soy sauce and wasabi amid the bookshelves and tables piled with literature. Behind a desk sits a man with his feet up, reading a book. Kind of Blue plays elegantly from a speaker. A real literati space.

You all have a press? asks Pyramus, standing before the desk.

The bespectacled man raises his gaze for a moment to look at Pyramus.

What's that?

Do you have a press here?

What do you mean?

Do you have a press? Do you publish books?

Oh, says the man, a look of comprehension tightening his pupils. Books. Not really. Leaflets, maybe. Pamphlets kind of.

He peels the corner of a page from his book and turns it over with a quiet hiss from the paper.

Anything specific? asks Pyramus.

Ummm… magic, mainly. Literature that deals in the instruction and performance of magic.

Like magic tricks?

Ya… well, no. Not tricks, perse. More like the attempt to achieve supernatural qualities from natural beings.

Oh, says Pyramus, turning to look down the long rows of bookshelves that extend to the back of the store. Thisbe has disappeared, somewhere. Beside the desk is a curved stairway that leads down to the basement, and at the back of the store is another set of stairs that goes up to the top floor.

Fifty fifty, says the man, beginning to read again from his book.

What's that?

She could be in the basement, or she could be upstairs.

Pyramus follows the curved staircase down to the basement, his hand lightly trailing along the rail that bows and bends downward. He finds himself in a dim space, cluttered with books, among which a small desk lamp illuminates a table top further back. At the table sits a woman hunched over a block of linoleum, a chisel gripped tightly in her hand, with which she peels long layers of linocut that curl and spiral like dried leaves on the floor around her.

Pyramus approaches cautiously, knocking into a few columns of stacked books that teeter precariously over his head, until he is gazing over the shoulder of the woman, and he can see the image that is carved into the piece of linoleum; a snarling wolf's head, the fur of which transforms into oak leaves at the base of its neck with two human hands reaching out, fingers spread.

Whazzat? says Pyramus over the woman's shoulder, causing her to jump in fright.

Spinning on her stool, the woman brandishes her tool like a weapon and even thrusts it towards Pyramus, catching his bare arm with the v shaped chisel, peeling a sliver of skin that now hangs pale and slightly translucent from the sharp metal.

Damn, says Pyramus, holding his hand against his forearm where a trickle of blood has begun to form. I didn't mean to scare you.

The woman takes him to a sink where he washes the cut with soap and water and then dries it with a paper towel. She produces a small vial of super glue, and, smoothing the piece of skin that lies crinkled like paper on the chisel, she pastes it back into place onto Pyramus's arm.

Is this sanitary? he says, wincing slightly as she touches his arm, although there is no pain from the wound. I mean medically speaking. I mean I've never seen anyone glue skin back in place.

The woman is a foot shorter than Pyramus, and she has straight silver hair, although the relatively tight skin around her face puts her age somewhere between thirty and forty.

Are you supposed to be down here? she says, returning to her perch on the stool, taking up her chisel, and carving deep grooves into the howling face of the wolf.

Oh, says Pyramus, I don't know. I was just looking for my girlfriend.

Before him, in the very back of the room, is a large press, a structure of iron and wood that expands outward and upward into the obscured light of the desk lamp. A big hydraulic cylinder holds a steel plate above the base of the press, and as

Pyramus pumps the handle protruding from the structure, the piston begins to extend downward, lowering the steel plate that is attached to it.

Please don't touch that, says the woman, not looking up from her work.

Oh, I'm sorry. This is pretty neat. The man upstairs says you all print pamphlets on magic. About how to do magic, I guess. Is that right?

The woman doesn't answer. Around the base of the press lie different illustrations printed on paper, and Pyramus leafs through them, examining each one, and then says, I guess you're the illustrator? For the pamphlets I mean?

But again, the woman doesn't answer, and Pyramus leaves her to her work, climbing the stairs back up to the ground floor. On the top floor, meanwhile, Thisbe is curled on a couch in a corner nook, reading a pamphlet on the practice of magic. It says that the supernatural exists in a plane outside of the human senses, but that, with practice, supernatural senses can be developed. Some precocious practitioners of magic are even born attuned to supernatural qualities.

Thisbe feels a deep stirring in her being at these words. And she is pretty sure it isn't just the sushi, although she does lean slightly to the side and lets a fart slip out, a quiet reverberation clapping her butt cheeks. Immediately, her stomach feels better, and she settles deeper into the cushions of the couch to read the rest of her pamphlet. It talks about a 13th century magician who was able to preserve his consciousness in a tree, and, through the subsequent centuries, transfer into different beings until, in 1997, he opened a bookstore on the corner of 39th and Ball street in Kansas City.

Downstairs, Pyramus finds a mechanical typewriter sitting on a shelf in a cutout in the back wall. A compact model with round keys, he lets his finger fall on a tab and he watches as a slender metal arm rises and presses its dark face against a light sheet of paper, and then fall back quietly into its slot. Pyramus looks closely at the image now printed on the paper, although it doesn't correspond to any letter in the alphabet, not any derived from the Greek, anway.

Please don't touch that, says the voice of the man at the desk, although from behind the shelves of books, he can't see Pyramus and Pyramus can't see him.

Sorry he says.

He follows the narrow stairwell that leads upstairs, in the wooden wall of which is another cutout, this one covered over with glass. Behind the glass is a garish red light that shines on a scene of figurines, seemingly stranded on an island, around which tosses a stormy sea. Pyramus remains enthralled for a moment, studying the characters, and then he climbs the rest of the way up the stairs.

He finds Thisbe in her nook and sits down next to her, cuddling close so he can see the pamphlet. It is only a few pages, printed on red paper with blue ink. On the front is an illustration of a large donut, only in place of the frosting there is a layer of writhing maggots.

Isn't this place amazing? says Pyramus, adjusting Thisbe's feet on the couch, which she has tucked beneath her, so that he can cradle her ass.

It says here that the best use of magic is the subversion of illegitimate authority, says Thisbe, running her finger along a line of text in the pamphlet. Do you know what that is?

No, says Pyramus. I don't. What is it?

It's any kind of authority that is derived from the use of force or bribery, and not from the will of the people whom it governs.

Where did you learn that?

It says it in this pamphlet.

When they leave the bookstore, the pregnant spring air has released its heavy load, and the water hits the streets and rebounds in little fountains like marbles falling from the sky. Thisbe and Pyramus walk hand in hand through the rain as if in a trance, letting the water soak them, watching as the clean white petals are knocked from the spring blossoms on the trees, falling on the sidewalk like snow. People clear 39th street before them, ducking into the bars and restaurants that line the street, peering out at through the windows at the poor souls left to soak in the downpour.

At their apartment, they enjoy lovemaking that is as intense as the downpour outside, fingers gripping, tongues searching, and legs shaking. They are left motionless in the sheets, filling their lungs with air, stinking, lacking the strength even to wipe the fluids that now drip from their stomachs and legs. Nine months later, Thisbe is lying on her back in a hospital bed, legs flung upward, and Pyramus watches as she pushes from her stretched birth canal, not a child, but a pamphlet, inscribed with the following stories that appear in this book.

The Nelson Atkins Museum of Miracles

The day before spring break, Mrs. Wright takes her eleventh grade world history class to the Nelson Atkins Museum of Art, to see the Egyptian, Greek, and Roman artifacts housed there. She teaches at East High School, on Van Brunt boulevard, and the students have just a short bus ride west through the city to get to the museum.

When the bus parks along the street that fronts the museum, the students spill out onto the sidewalk and then run up into the sculpture garden, a shaded area with high trees overhanging a brick walking path and lined with a stone wall. The garden follows a gentle rise and then opens onto a long, manicured mall, the bright green grass of which is decorated with two enormous badminton shuttlecocks, each one suspended in leaning angles as if caught forever in the act of play.

The students spread out onto the wide lawn like a solution in a suspension, and Mrs. Wright waves them up towards the big building that sits like a capstone atop the long sloping lawn.

To the museum! she cries out in a voice that carries a very small distance in a very open space.

The stone structure is massive, its centerpiece fronted with tall marble columns, flanked with wide wings on each side, the stone of which is engraved with giant letters and images. The students climb the high stone steps and sit and stand about like bright laundry stranded on a beach, the sunshine bathing them and the stone in glaring colors. Some of the students hold out their phones and take selfies, some take pictures of the sweeping view of scenery below them, and some chase each other up and down the steps, laughing loudly.

Taleea sits on the top step, leaning back on a stone column with her arm propped up on her knee.

Take my picture, Anarae, she says, handing a girl her phone.

How come you never wear jeans, says Anarae, taking the phone and pointing its camera towards Taleea.

I do too wear jeans. Just take my picture and make me look good.

Down the steps, Javon runs back and forth on the landing between the first and second set of steps with a doll in his hand. The doll is nondescript, made of a bit of cotton sewn up in a brown fabric, and its legs and arms flop limply as he runs with it. As Mrs. Wright comes up the steps, she holds out her hand to Javon, and he hands the doll to her. She gives it back to Esther, who is standing in the shadow of a monolithic sculpture, away from the other students. Esther takes the doll and clinches it to her chest.

Standing at the top of the steps, dwarfed by the massive columns around her and the high entranceways behind her, Mrs. Wright calls out to her students like a high priest before the temple.

Ladies and gentlemen, please, she cries out, holding her arms aloft, please can I have your attention. The tour through the museum will begin in just a moment. When we get inside,

I need you to be on your best behaviour. Please give our tour guide your full attention, and be respectful. There will be a reward afterwards for those who comply.

Is there a bathroom inside? says Mary Grace. I gotta poop!

Grace!

What? You want me to lie and tell these people I gotta tinkle?

Filing through the entryway, the doors of which are massive bronze entablatures engraved with scenes from Greek mythology, the students gather in a large hall and take in the sights around them. Their voices and laughter echo from the marble floors and high ceilings, held aloft with rows of pillars. An awkward man in a suit coat and baggy trousers stands before them and, after a brief introduction, he leads them through the hall, into the wing where are housed the sarcophagus' of ancient Egyptian monarchs.

But one does not follow, and she creeps instead into the opposite wing where the walls are strewn with paintings of lifelike scenes and persons. Esther finds herself standing before a portrait of a vase and flowers with insects crawling on their petals. The botanical picture is almost scientific in its detail, and Esther holds her doll up so it, too, can examine the green stems of the flowers, the pale petals streaked with purple, and the delicate bees climbing among the pink pistils. But Esther's doll lacks eyes with which to view the painting; in fact it lacks a face altogether, as the brown fabric of its head is blank, with only a small tuft of thread on the top for hair.

From the corner of her eye, Esther feels someone watching her. Without looking around, Esther begins to walk through the gallery, walking past a large stone lion, the snout of which has eroded into a toothless grin. For a moment, she hides behind the statue, peeking out from behind the tail and looking at the security guard who is watching her. Then she runs.

As the paintings on the walls begin to blur from realism into an impressionistic river of running color, Esther hears the squawk of a walkie talkie behind her and she ducks into the corridor of a stairwell. The stairs take her up to the second floor, and with the change in elevation, Esther finds she has been transported into a different civilization. Native American masks and headdresses hang behind glass cabinets, along with the skins of animals and weapons made from wood and stone.

In the eastern civilization wing, a security guard almost corners her in the fourth arm of a wooden Vishnu, but she slips away and stumbles into a life size replica of a buddhist temple. Immediately, she is taken to China, in the evening, where a perfect purple sun weaves through raveled ivy onto the rough stone floor. Buddha is front and center, seated on a stone pillar, meditating. When he hears Esther's footsteps shuffling on the stone, he opens his eyes and looks at her.

Are you lost? he asks, slightly adjusting his crossed legs on the pillar.

Esther wears a black head band, speckled with dandruff as it holds her hair back from her face.

Probably, she says, still clinching the doll to her chest.

Would you like me to help you find your way home?

I don't really have one.

Ah, says the Buddha. And what is your doll's name?

It's not a doll says Esther. It's my son. His name's Rae Rae.

I apologize. Even after a millennia of practice, I still miss the life force in the smallest of beings. Would you like to meditate with me?

Climbing onto the pillar beside him, Esther folds her legs and takes the seated position of the Buddha. As she meditates, Rae Rae begins to stir in her lap. From the brown fabric around his head, eye sockets are scooped out like clay and filled with puddles of color. Through his eyes, visions of bodily instincts enter his mind; images of slimy flesh engorged with blood and nerves; the smells of fluids and orifices sour and rank; limbs enmeshed one over the other.

He climbs down from his mother's lap and walks around the temple, stretching his limbs and torso. The room is quiet, as is the museum that lies just beyond the arched stone entrance, and Rae Rae listens to his foot falls as he explores the space. There are ancient scrolls on display, marked with fine brush strokes that fatten and thin out and then disappear. There are images, too, of temples overlooking waterfalls and wildly feathered birds painted on the scrolls.

When Rae Rae looks back at his mother, she is still perfectly poised in her meditative pose next to Buddha. Esther is so still, in fact, that when Rae Rae reaches out and touches her, he feels only the smooth, cool texture of stone.

There is a security guard waiting for Rae Rae when he leaves the temple and he is escorted ceremoniously back to the school tour. He finds his class gaggled before a piece of ancient Greek pottery with a naked man painted on it. When Mrs. Wright sees Rae Rae, she says, We'll talk after the tour.

On the bus ride back to East High School, the students are allowed to breathe freely and play, freed from the confines of the museum. Their shouts and screams and the music from their phones carry throughout the bus and out the windows. Sliding down the pane of glass next to him, Rae Rae takes in the warm spring air, thrilled at the chance to suck at the nipple of life.

And who knows what new life will be created in the throes of springtime? What new beings will be birthed to crawl and walk the surface of the earth, and make their impressions in the dirt, or in the short scrolls of human history?

Daddy

The Autozone on Independence avenue stays busy with a steady stream of the bereft, the stranded, the vehicularly cursed. Long lines of those poor souls, whose hearts have been broken by ancient machinery, extend to the back of the store and wind around the aisles. Chevy Cavaliers, Oldsmobile Cutlass', Ford Tempos, Dodge Neons; machines that long ago have passed their day of usefulness but are strung along, part by part, tire after tire, until they are no more than rusty spectres limping through the streets not by gasoline but by the sheer will power of those who drive them.

Jenae and Lovelady stand in line together, waiting to make their sacrifice at the altar of those fickle vehicular gods. Jenae wears a stocking cap that sits folded and collapsed, hardly covering her hair. Lovelady wears a set of canvas coveralls that are smeared with dirt and grease. As they wait, they watch the long line of automotive sinners filter one by one up to the counter and receive their benediction. Some curse their fates. Some cry. Some throw the old broken parts to the floor, where a thick rubber mat protects the tile from years of abuse.

In his grease stained hand, Lovelady holds a hunk of cast iron, from the hollow core of which tubing protrudes like arms and legs. Within the formed body, he spins a splined shaft that turns freely.

This gear spins, he says, and pressurizes the housing. That's what sends the oil up to the journals.

I don't care how it works, says Jenae, so long as it fixes my truck. You know I get depressed when my truck doesn't run. It wears my nerves.

It is a full twenty three minutes before they reach the counter. When they get there, there is an old man with tired eyes behind the counter sitting on a stool. He passes an unhurried look across the faces of Lovelady and Jenae.

You know they don't pay me enough for this, says the old man. All day it's been like this. We ain't had a break since we opened. I know you ain't drippin oil all over my counter, now.

From the sprawling passageways of the housing, a black substance leaks and spills onto the counter, and Lovelady smears it with the sleeve of his coveralls.

Ah shit boss, I didn't see that. My bad.

What's it out of? says the old man, beginning to peck at the keyboard of a computer with a crooked yellowing finger.

Eighty nine Ford pickup.

What engine's it got in it?

Four nine. Straight six.

It's my truck, says Jenae.

The old man clucks and shakes his head again.

I got two pumps in stock. One's fifty, one's a hundred. Which one you want?

What's the difference? says Jenae.

I don't have the slightest. Probably the same thing, one just tricks people into paying twice the price.

You ain't got a hundred dollars anyways, says Lovelady. What are you worrying for?

The old man behind the counter slides off his stool, grimacing, and begins a slow limp to the shelves behind him. Jenae gets out her cash, and then the old man limps back to the counter and sets the box onto the countertop.

Be 52.99 with tax, he says.

Jenae sets the dollars on the counter and slides them across. They seem to smear a trail across the surface, as if the very paper oozes filth from its pores. The old man takes them up in his fingers and peels them apart, separating the bills into sheaves of grease and oil.

Good luck with your truck, he says.

Ain't no luck to it, says Lovelady.

Outside, the avenue thrives with movement. A bus stops and people get on and off. A woman struggles to carry two heavy bags of laundry down the sidewalk. Another man pulls a tarp loaded with a pile of rags behind him. The rags pick up in the wind and blow into the street.

Jenae and Lovelady follow an alley back through the neighborhood, through the houses that slouch in the shifting silt and dissolve into formless piles of rafters and siding. The windows seem lifeless, hollow and empty. Behind the fences that line the alley are dogs that bark at nothing; barking at the footsteps and voices that invade their little worlds behind the cobbled fences of plywood and siding and corrugated tin.

They enter a gap in a chain link fence that has been cut and rolled back and then they come into the backyard of an old house, beside which sits Jenae's truck. Tommy sits in an old lawn chair beside a grill that sizzles with hot dogs. Over the back door of the house behind him, a piece of plywood covers the frame and reads in spray paint, New Owner Tommy.

On the grate of the grill, the plump hot dogs blister and burst. Lovelady pinches one up in his fingers and bites it, cupping the hot meat below his tongue. Jenae slides beneath the truck where the belly of the engine hangs slashed open, its guts exposed in a gruesome display of mechanical gore. The oil pan sits on the ground and above it are the journals of the main bearings and the crankshaft, poking down like a ribbed torso deskinned.

Lovelady, says Jenae, holding a gnarled hand out from beneath the truck, hand me that pump.

She feels the hard iron placed in her fingers and brings it to her chest, holding it up to the bottom of the engine. Sliding the flanges up to the surfaces where they mate with the engine, she pushes the oil pump into place, but the bolt holes won't line up. From the exposed crankshaft and bearings, black oil still drips onto Jenae below.

Lovelady, get down here and gimme a hand.

Lovelady's big head appears beneath the truck and then he, too, scoots on his back beneath the motor, his thick torso barely fitting beneath the truck. His big hand covers the pump and then he presses upward and it pops into place, flush with its mount.

You just need some muscle on them bones, he says, passing the bolts to Jenae.

Her little fingers screw the bolts up into the threads of the housing and then Lovelady hands her the ratchet and she tightens them down. They fit the oil pan up and over the naked crankshaft and then fill it with fresh oil.

Turn it over, Lovelady, says Jenae.

The old engine winds into life, struggling, stuttering and coughing for air. It turns and turns, those big pistons shoving through their cylinders and pushing and pulling the air in great vacuums through the motor. But when Lovelady releases his stranglehold on the key, nothing happens. The backyard goes quiet.

Ain't firing, says Tommy.

Standing up from his chair, he shuffles over to the truck. He climbs up the bumper and reaches over the engine, taking off the valve cover cap.

Go on and turn it over.

The engine rumbles with Tommy on top of it and then it quits and he climbs back down, wiping his hands clean on his pants.

Camshaft ain't turning over, he says. Timing belt's broke.

Jenae stares over at Lovelady, who's head pokes out from behind the windshield.

Timing belt? says Lovelady. I thought I heard that oil pump knocking.

I oughtta kick your ass, Lovelady, says Jenae.

She leaves the backyard and walks around the old house that stumbles and spills its guts into the streets. A violent protrusion of garbage and furniture ejects from the front door and flows like a river of filth out into the yard.

The sun now drops in a long steady arc over the neighborhood, the shadows climbing higher on the faces of the houses, the dark corners deepening into pockets of visceral night. Jenae shivers as two big dogs cross the street, one brown and one black, their heavy skulls shrouded in folds of thick skin; great gouts of foam dribbling from their ponderous jaws.

And who can say where she goes among that network of uncharted labyrinths? Those places of the city that seem to fall off the map and defy zip code, taxation and law. She finds herself knocking at a door, a white door that is locked and ungiving. From an upper window, a dark head extends through the frame and looks down at her.

Who is it?

Mamita, I need my daddy. I'm lost.

Go away, says the head. I'm not helping you tonight.

Mamita please! My truck ain't runnin!

The head disappears and after a moment the white door that stands closed before Jenae opens. The woman that appears in the doorway is spectrally thin, a mere shadow in the dark.

You can only come in if you will take a shower, she says. My incense can't hide your stink.

The passageway inside the house is narrow and lit with a thousand candles. The shelves on which they sit and give their flickering light are filled with statues of Mary and Jesus, Buddha, and the figure of Death cast as a skeleton holding a scythe. From a cubby hole within the labyrinth, a gaggle of children laugh and run across their path, and the woman says, Go to your room. I have a visitor.

Jenae follows the woman through the winding corridor and then up a staircase into another hallway. The woman guides her into the bathroom and then disappears for a moment into the cloistered darkness. When she reappears, she is holding a towel and a washcloth in her hands, on top of which lies a folded pair of clean underwear.

Don't forget to wash your ass, she says.

Jenae strips off the jeans and sweatshirt that are soaked in oil, even the old stocking cap that somehow still clings to its tentative hold on her hair. Her thin frame protrudes through her skin in sharp points and angles that speak of an existence ground in the hard millstones of utilitarianism.

Stepping into the hot stream of water that pours down from the showerhead, she can feel the layers of dirt and grease begin to dissolve on her skin and run into the bottom of the tub, forming a dark river that drains and disappears.

Is he here? she says, now smelling the incense that is burning somewhere in the bathroom.

He's here, says the woman's voice.

The inside of the curtain is decorated with a life size image of Death, its skull wearing gaping eye sockets of nothingness.

Hi daddy, says Jenae.

Hey baby, says a man's voice, the tone sounding slightly muffled and distant.

My truck's not running.

Is the camshaft turning?

No.

Get that timing belt changed.

I'm gonna fix it. I don't let anybody else drive it. I know you gave it to me. I ain't forgot that.

I know that, baby. I know it ain't easy. You do you. I love you, I'm gonna watch over you and take care of you. You'll get it fixed.

The water in the bottom of the tub now drains clean and clear and Jenae turns the handles to shut it off. She pats herself down with the towel and dresses and then follows the winding corridors back through the house. The woman follows her and, standing in the doorway, she calls out to Jenae.

The spirits of the dead are carried on in the souls of the living, she says.

Jenae traces her steps back through the labyrinthian neighborhoods, and ducks once more through the peeled back chain link fence. The neighborhood is dark and quiet, a few street lights gathering enough energy to spill a feeble orange light from their cracked mouths.

Opening the door of her truck, she climbs into the long bench seat and stretches her small frame across the ripped fabric that spills and leaks bits of the foam cushion. As she lies there, she thinks about removing the front cover of the engine and changing the timing belt. She thinks about changing the water pump while she's in there, and the extra coolant she will need to buy.

The old truck that passed into her possession is aging and getting harder and harder to maintain. She often thinks about letting go of the truck and releasing the burden it represents, but the mechanical workings of those pieces seem to grip her heart like the spirit of the dead that haunt the living.

Onion Skin

The Kansas City police department shooting range is located in a deserted section of Coal Mine road. The road runs along the Blue river watershed, a shallow area of lagoons and marshland, most of it contaminated by years of use as a dumping ground for the nearby steel plant. The area for the range is hacked out of a dense woodland, and consists of a few low sheds and trailers and a high berm lined with targets in the shape of human torsos. Rising above the little clearing is a wooden tower constructed to give the policemen practice at shooting from high vantage points.

On a clear night with ample moonlight, Lucky and Donna sit on this elevated platform and shoot heroin together. Perhaps because it is dark and deserted, or perhaps to spite the men and women who go there to prepare to shoot people, they have chosen this vantage point at which to break the law.

As they plunge those sacred solutions deep into one another, they laugh about those men and women sharing this space with them; the officers that take aim in the daylight with their weapons drawn as if a horde of hardened criminals is issuing from that high berm to charge them. Firing pistols and rifles grooved to meet the shapes of their hands; their barrels kicking back and then leveling again, ready to recoil when the trigger is pulled.

Lucky and Donna lean back against the railing of the platform for a moment and nod. They can see the range below them, the concrete tunnels and the low netting set out for the policemen to navigate as they shoot; the water of the Blue river shining among the trees behind the berm; the smokestacks of the steel plant poking up black on the sky. Lucky lets the euphoria wash over her and then feels the calm set in as Donna slouches up against her and settles into her armpit. Donna's hair still smells like shampoo as Lucky rests her cheek on Donna's head.

I love you babe, says Donna, looking up into Lucky's eyes. You know that? I love you so much. What am I without you, babe? You can't leave me. Don't ever leave me. I'm a pimple on this world's ass. You know that? And you love me. How did I get so lucky to find you?

Lucky lets her fingers disappear in Donna's hair and then she slowly massages her scalp. The noise from the highway filters through the trees, the hum of distant cars mingling with the croak of tree frogs.

Why do you get so emotional when you get high? says Lucky. You have to talk like god herself is here with us, ordaining this moment as holy. I love you. We don't have to constantly reaffirm our love to each other. I got you. I'm not going anywhere.

But I want you to know how much I need you, Lucky. I'm nothing without you. You know that, right? I cry when I think about something happening to you. I don't know what I would do. No one has ever loved me like you do, Lucky.

When the high begins to loosen its grip on their limbs and their thoughts, they gather themselves and descend the steps of the high wooden tower. They pass a few low sheds and trailers sitting indistinctly in the dark and then they come to a cattle gate flanked by concrete barriers at the entrance of the range. Lucky helps Donna climb the gate and then she climbs it herself and they go out through the night along Coal Mine road.

The road is flanked by dense woods on each side until it dips below an old railroad bridge and turns sharply to follow alongside the highway. Beneath the wooden trestles of the bridge, Donna stops and takes in her arms the width of one of the supports.

I wonder how old this bridge is, she says. Do you think any trains still cross it? What if a train comes across it right now, and the bridge collapses? Do you think anybody would find us? Would anybody look?

People are gonna notice a train wreck, says Lucky.

She runs her hand along one of the big bolt heads that protrude from the railroad ties, its long shaft piercing two supports and holding them together.

Ya but if nobody knows we're here, how would they know to look for us? Like if they were cleaning up the wreck, and they were picking up the metal with a big crane and they just scooped us up and took us to the junkyard.

They walk in the middle of the road, holding hands, until a car comes and separates them, Lucky going to one side and Donna the other. The bright headlights of the car create a blinding cascade of light, into which Lucky and Donna stare and blink as they watch it pass. The car takes the curve beneath the bridge and then its lights disappear somewhere in the thick woods.

Who was it? says Donna as they converge once again in the road.

I think it was the pope, says Lucky. He's on his way to dump the bodies he keeps in his closet.

No. It's my father. He likes to drive past me in my dreams and pretend like he cares about me.

The road runs up through the Leed's industrial park, and they pass an automotive junkyard and a metal recycling facility before they come to the steel plant. The dark building is massive, sprawling across acres of cement. The cylindrical exhaust stacks run along its high walls and protrude into the air, giving the building the look of some ship stranded in the concrete when the river changed its course.

I want to live in this building, says Donna, looking up at the high windows that glare squarely in the walls. I want to crawl up in one of those exhaust stacks and sleep forever. Don't you think it's warm and cozy up there? Like no one would ever bother you?

Lucky and Donna cut through the plant's parking lot, walking between stacked storage containers and semi-trailers unhitched and headless. Tufts of grass grow up through the gravel beneath their feet. They follow a set of railroad tracks that lead inside the building where docks have been set up to unload the cargo from the cars; great chains with iron hooks hanging from pulleys high overhead, and pigeons shuttling in the rafters. Lucky and Donna are dwarfed in the immense space, with a shower of moonlight passing through the windows, creating dark shadows and pale protrusions.

On the other side, they exit out the back of the building and cross another parking lot, entering a dilapidated neighborhood. A big German shepherd stalks them behind a chain link fence, its fierce bark echoing back from the steel plant in the empty night.

I think that dog is lonely, says Donna. I think we ought to let it out so it can run around and find some friends.

I think it is out, says Lucky.

As they come to the end of the fence, they realize there is no side to it, and the dog stands uninhibited before them.

Oh shit, says Donna, looking at the dog's jowls snapping as it barks.

But the dog holds its line before the imaginary fence, as if the chain link extends on, as if the world for that dog does not extend past those boundaries. Walking on, Lucky and Donna pass an empty church and a few more yards that wash up to little houses, and then they come to a small business front that lines the road. In a window that has the blinds drawn down, an open sign glows red and they walk through the entrance of a recessed door.

You know what sounds good? says Donna, sitting down on a stool at the diner counter. Onions. I mean a whole heap of onions. Doesn't that sound amazing?

Before them on the counter is a chrome napkin holder and a bottle of ketchup and mustard with a couple of menus pinched between them. Lucky takes up a menu and turns it over in her hands.

Yes, says Lucky, looking at the stained plastic. Onions and pie sound amazing right now.

The diner is just one room with a counter and a few booths and a kitchen in the back. Behind the counter, a silent television shows a black and white western atop a drink cooler. The stainless steel shelves beside it are stacked with pitchers and cups and mugs full of silverware, and from a dusty radio in the corner, the distorted voice of Dwight Yoakam crackles softly.

What are you two knuckleheads having? says the waitress, coming from the back and setting two glasses of water on the counter.

Have I ever told you how much I love this woman? says Donna, putting her arm around Lucky and pulling her close.

She is everything to me. My whole world. Whatever she wants, anything on the menu, I want her to have. Because she deserves it. And there is only one thing I love as much as her. Onions. Can you put an entire onion in the oven for about thirty minutes with some salt and butter and bring it out to me?

The waitress holds a pen in her hand, the end of which she taps against a protrusive canine tooth. Around the curled edges of her ears are tattooed lines connected by dots. Along the cuticles of her fingernails, too, is tattooed the same design.

Ya, I can do that she says, writing onion on her notepad and circling it. And what do you want?

Lucky looks up at the chalkboard on the wall behind the counter, on which is written Pie $3.00 - Pecan, Banana Cream, Coconut Cream, Chocolate Peanut Butter Cream.

I'll have a piece of Banana Cream pie, says Lucky. No, wait. Chocolate Peanut Butter Cream.

The waitress disappears behind the wall in the back, which has a doorway and a horizontal window that is hung with paper tickets. Behind the window, a man in a greasy apron moves in subtle and hidden motions.

I'm gonna go to the bathroom, says Donna, getting up off her stool and then leaning over and kissing Lucky on the head. Save some pie for me.

Lucky turns on her stool and watches the silent television, on the screen of which a black and white baby doll is mechanically blinking and opening and closing its mouth. There is a man on screen, as well, holding the baby doll, and he is looking intently into the doll's face as if he would understand what the doll is saying. Lucky thinks this is strange as dolls aren't supposed to talk, but she can't tell exactly what is going on as the sound is off. The doll's face begins to move more organically, its lips and eyelids becoming more supple and less mechanical.

As the camera zooms in on the dolls' face, it continues to move its eyes and mouth and even its nostrils now take definition and flare open and shut. Lucky realizes the face is becoming human, and not just any human, but it is beginning to resemble Donna's face. And then it is Donna on the television, and she is screaming at Lucky, trying to get her attention.

When Lucky looks away from the television, she sees that the cook is leaning in the service window, watching her. She looks back at the screen, but now there is a commercial on the television, one of those late night ads for lawyer services.

You ever seen him before? says the cook, watching the lawyer on the television through the service window. My wife works for him. She's his secretary. He works out every morning in the gym. She says she can hear him screaming from her office. She says he changes in the office bathroom and leaves his dirty undies on the floor. Can you imagine that?

But when Lucky looks back at the television, Donna's face is once again on the screen, only this time her eyes are rolled back in her head.

Do you see that? Lucky asks the cook. Do you see that girl on the television?

But the cook has his back turned now and Lucky can see him handling an onion, the outer layers of which are beginning to break apart in his hand like old wrapping paper. Getting up from her stool, Lucky walks to the back of the diner and looks through the doorway in which Donna had disappeared.

Is the bathroom back here? she asks the cook.

Ya, to the right, he says.

Through the doorway is another sitting area, with more tables and booths. The room is dark, unused. In an alcove in the wall is the entrance to the bathroom and, walking past a serving cart laden with pitchers and styrofoam cups, Lucky knocks on the door. She doesn't hear anything.

When the cook takes the onion out of the oven, it slumps softly on the baking sheet, its bottom flattened and sides collapsed. A bit of dark pith bubbles out from its heart and spills down its outer layer, crystallising on the hot metal pan. He lifts it off the baking sheet and sets it on a plate, indenting the soft body where his fingers pinched it up. As the butter melts into its opened core, he sprinkles a bit of salt on it and then sets the plate in the service window, next to the piece of pie. From the steaming onion, waves of heat rise and distort the air in the small diner, softening the hard knots of reality with which the world is held together.

Find Your Marbles at Moon Marble, Bonner Springs, KS

On the banks of the Kansas river, dynamited deep into the rocky hillside, is a cave system that has been converted into a cold storage facility. The cave was originally dynamited by the Army Corps of Engineers for the storage of sensitive materials, but after so many years it was sold into private hands. Now, a steady stream of semi trucks travel up and down the little road that leads out to the facility, loaded with frozen fruit, vegetables, meat, dairy products, and anything else that needs to be kept cold as it awaits distribution across the country.

The cave extends almost a half mile into the hillside, and the staggered rock vaults high overhead, streaked with piping that carries the refrigerant deep into the cave, dripping dirty droplets of condensation like a soot filled rain forest. The condensation pools in the depressions of the concrete below, creating a dark river that traces through the cave.

Bud and Unk work deep inside these caves, shuttling heavy boxes of frozen meat from stack to stack, layered with coveralls and coats and gloves to protect themselves from the blasts of arctic air that pour out from the cooling fans. Inside the freezers, which are huge rooms filled with aisles and aisles of stacked frozen goods, the temperature is around 15 degrees with a wind chill from the fans that goes down to single digits.

Bud and Unk stand just outside the freezer, resting for a moment in the uncooled portion of the cave, which is a practically tropical 40 degrees. Along the ceiling, next to the refrigerant piping, hang bright halogen bulbs with metal housings that light the cave deep within its bowels.

Unk's nephew, who just started working in the cave, stands alongside them, his coat unzipped and his cold hands shoved into the warm pockets of his armpits.

Gotta work fast says Bud, wiping the condensation from the lenses of his glasses with his coat sleeve. Get in and get the hell out.

How many pallets we gotta stack?

More'n you can count, says Unk.

Inside the freezer, the three men get back to work, stacking pallets of frozen meat that the forklift drivers will then pick up and carry out to the docks and load onto the waiting semi trucks. After each pallet is completed, they each stand about eight feet tall, and Bud and Unk and Neffy have to wrap them around with rolls of cling wrap so that they don't come apart.

Neffy holds the roll with both hands and circles a pallet, pulling the cling wrap tight as he goes. He works from the bottom up, double wrapping it, and about halfway up he begins to feel dizzy, circling and circling, and suddenly his breakfast is in his throat, Lucky Charms cereal, hardly digested. Dropping the roll and leaning over, he vomits a burst of whole grain and marshmallow onto the ground, where it almost instantaneously freezes to the cold concrete.

You have Lucky Charms this morning? says Bud, nudging a pink marshmallow with his boot.

Yup.

You oughta try Fruit Loops. Don't come back up as easy.

At lunch, they make the long journey out of the cave, their feet tired and sore from walking on the hard concrete all morning. Unk's back hurts, Bud's tooth hurts, and Neffy isn't sure he wants to live anymore. When they reach the docks, they shed their coats and coveralls and stumble into the sunlight, squint eyed, still partially frozen, letting the warmth cook them to the bone. The car, with the windows up, is a cool 120 degrees and they sit inside and ruminate like three potatoes in an oven.

Just down the road from the storage facility is Bonner Springs, a little satellite community of Kansas City along the river. With Unk driving, they make their way into town and stop at the local Dairy Queen, at the drive thru window of which, a worker leans out and hands Unk a bag of burgers.

Y'all might wanna spray some potpourri in your car says the worker, giving Unk three milkshakes as well. I can smell your weed through the window.

Nah says Unk, passing the milkshakes around the car. We work in a cave, smells like that.

Listen, I don't care where you smoke it. I'm just lettin you know I can smell it.

No no. The cold storage facility. We pack meat down there.

Ya. I don't know what the hell that means, but ya'll be careful drivin home.

They sit in the Dairy Queen parking lot, quiet, not talking, eating cow meat and ice cream like zombies at a brain buffet. Across the street is an odd little building, a low structure painted gunmetal gray with a brick front and a long metal warehouse that extends out the back. Standing over the structure is a high sign with a smiling moon that says Moon Marble.

What is that place? says Neffy, dipping two steaming french fries into his milkshake and shoveling the ice cream into his mouth.

Some kinda toy store, looks like, says Bud.

Along the top of the building are paintings of more smiling moons and a big flag that says OPEN!

I'm gonna check it out.

We ain't got time says Unk. We gotta get back to work.

Fuck that place, says Neffy. Ten dollars an hour ain't worth freezin to death for. Lemme out.

Crossing the street, still holding his milkshake and slurping a thick glob of ice cream up the straw, Neffy walks past a few spinning pinwheels and enters Moon Marble. Inside is a toy store extraordinaire, wall to wall shelves of handmade marbles all sizes and colors, board games, chess sets, masks, puppets and all kinds of glass art hanging from the ceiling.

Neffy sticks his hand into the gaping mouth of a face shaped barrell and claws up a handful of marbles, rolling the smooth orbs in his palm. Blues and reds and yellows lace through the glass in delicate strands, twining together in intricate patterns. Some even have scenes within the glass, figures that resemble people and animals.

There doesn't seem to be anyone else in the store and Neffy takes his time examining each oddity, picking them up and setting them back down, taking occasional long sucks of ice cream. His favorite is the jacob's ladder, which he spends an inordinate amount of time with, watching the blocks flip over, changing color, direction and texture in a seemingly endless display of magic.

As he plays, engrossed in the simple yet illusive contraption, Neffy doesn't hear the creature come up behind him, a hideous monster with red eyeballs and jet black hair that twists upward into stiff strands as sharp as knives.

When he catches the monster in the corner of his eye, Neffy screams and drops his milkshake, splattering a semi solid substance across the floor for the second time that day. The monster laughs loudly, and then peels its face from its head, revealing an old man with terrible breath whose eyebrows leap up his forehead with delight.

Oh god! he chokes out amid his laughter. Oh god! I gotchoo! I gotchoo! You shoulda seen you! Oh god!

And he even steps in the spilled milkshake with his boot as he laughs.

Outside, Bud and Unk drive back to the cave, gearing up to go back into the freezers and work. The work seems to go smoother without Neffy there, and before Bud and Unk realize it, a few hours have passed inside the freezer. The pallets they have completed stand tall and secure, solid boxes on the bottom, light boxes on top, a technique Unk has developed after watching numberless pallets topple over just outside the freezer due to careless forklift drivers. He had to restack them all.

It is a peculiar satisfaction seeing a job completed, something your own effort and knowledge has accomplished, even in repetitions of physical labor. Standing before the rows and rows of stacked pallets, neatly wrapped and secured, Bud and Unk take a moment to admire their work. But that rush of euphoria doesn't last long, because when Bud tugs on the rope switch that opens the freezer door, nothing happens.

Damn says Bud, tugging and tugging on the rope. The door won't open.

Somebody'll come, says Unk.

After waiting for so long, they try to pry the door open, but the solid metal structure is secure in its frame, sealing the cold air, along with Bud and Unk, inside the freezer. Then the bright lights, housed in their metal cones along the ceiling, go dark.

They forgot about us, says Bud. We're gonna freeze to death in here.

Unk starts to yell, screaming and pounding on the door. From somewhere behind them, deep in the cave, is a faint light, against which the stacked pallets rise up, although its distance is difficult to tell. They walk for what seems like an hour deeper into the cave, following the illusive light, although whether or not Bud and Unk are coming closer to it is hard to determine. Finally they reach the light, a single strand that illuminates an odd contraption of rope and wood that hangs down from somewhere up above.

What is this? says Bud, looking up into the hole in the ceiling in which the ladder disappears.

I think it goes up to the surface, says Unk.

Bud tries to climb the ladder, but the odd wooden blocks strung together with rope flip over awkwardly when he does, and he tumbles back into Unk's waiting arms. He attempts the climb again, this time more carefully, and when he reaches the level of the high ceiling, where the ladder begins to tunnel upward, he looks back down at Unk.

You coming? he calls.

Ain't no way I can get my fat ass up this goofy ladder.

You got any other options?

Unk looks around into the cold and darkness for a moment, and then he, too, begins to climb.

On the surface, in Moon Marble, the old man is demonstrating to Neffy how he forms the marbles, how he heats the colored rods of glass with a torch and mixes them together in the spherical iron cast. They are deep inside the warehouse that extends out the back of the toy store, and Moony talks excitedly as he waves the glowing torch around himself in the semi dark. Neffy watches him.

Creation is the highest calling of any person, says Mooney, wearing a pair of goofy goggles over his eyes as he feeds a ribbon of pliant glass into the mold. And glasswork is the highest form of creation. Don't take my word for it. You can see it with your own eyes. I can create whole worlds within these little glass marbles, microcosms of the vast universe in which we live. And it is my sincerest belief that our own universe is itself housed within a marble, just one among many that God carries around in his pocket, using us to play games with on the playground of life.

Meanwhile, beneath the earth, Bud and Unk reach the top of the ladder, having climbed through a tunnel of rock a hundred feet long. They exit through a little hole in the surface of the hillside and find themselves in a wooded stand that overlooks the river. Except around the hole, bubbling up among the trees, is a glass enclosure just big enough for Bud and Unk to stand up in.

You ever seen anything like this? says Bud, knocking on the glass with his knuckle.

Unk shakes his head.

And so, after a stint in the oven, Mooney cools the marble that he has just made in water and then sets the smooth orb in Neffy's palm. Neffy is dumbstruck at the detail of the scene within the marble.

How'd you do that? says Neffy, holding the marble up to look at it better. That looks just like Bud and Unk!

As Neffy sets his knuckles down on the ground and flicks the marble across the cement floor of the warehouse, Unk and Bud watch the world spin outside their glass enclosure like a gyroscope set into motion by the gods. When they look back down at the hole in the ground, the ladder is gone and there is no way to climb back down into the depths of darkness.

How did we get in here? says Bud.

I followed you, says Unk.

The Country Music Station Plays Soft

Lorna's Tax Service is run by Greg and Rudee Gourley, a husband and wife duo in the suburbs of Kansas City. Their office is a little one story house on a non descript cul-de-sac with other houses just like it. The only thing that gives it away as a place of business is a small sign next to the front door.

Greg is the certified tax accountant and Rudee runs the scheduling and paperwork. Over the years, their business expands, and they take on two additional employees to handle bookkeeping services.

When Johanna is first hired to work in the office, she is put off by the office's cloistered atmosphere. She has trouble breathing. During the interview process, she doesn't see Greg or Rudee, but speaks only with the secretary, Robin. She sits in front of her desk, trying not to let Robin catch her looking around. Above Robin on the wall is a mural identifying each of the seven deadly sins; each sin labeled with a modernist, abstract image.

No matter the conditions outside, the office is always kept at a humid 84 degrees, even though there never seems to be any air blowing from a heater or air conditioner. It is as if the piles and piles of paper around the walls, stacked to the ceiling, have provided a permanent insulation for the house. Often the office smells unsavory; smells of old, damp paper, damp skin and bad breath.

On her first day, Johanna is placed behind a desk with a computer that is almost hidden in a stack of folders packed with paper. She works all morning, and at noon, she gets up and asks Robin where the bathroom is.

Oh we don't have one, says Robin, not looking up from her work.

Johanna is a little confused, but she returns to her desk and continues to work. There is one front window in the office, and when the light outside begins to darken with sunset, there are only a few shaded lamps around the room that give light, along with the computer screens.

When do you all go home? Johanna asks Robin, over a stack of folders.

Oh we don't go home, says Robin.

You don't go home?

Not during tax season.

Johanna thinks for a minute. She is beginning to feel a little panicked, and the need to urinate is overwhelming.

Can I go home? she asks.

Of course!

Through the weeks, Johanna learns to adjust to the work-flow of tax season, and her first week's paycheck is so substantial, she is inspired to work even more. One night she even decides to spend the night, keeping a discreet silver pot beneath her desk for her slops.

One of her jobs in the office is to process the clients coming through for tax services, preparing all the paperwork and intake information before their one on one consultation with Greg. She has begun to notice something peculiar throughout the weeks, however. When the clients enter Greg's office, they don't come back out.

On the night she decides to stay and work late, she is determined to investigate this peculiarity. Around 2 am, when there is no sound inside or outside the office, Johanna leaves her desk and approaches the room into which the clients have disappeared.

Opening the door, she finds a room almost perfectly mirroring the one she is in, papers, copy machines, cabinets; only Greg sits behind the desk, instead of herself. He sleeps with his head on the desktop. Behind the desk, amid the stacks of loose paper, is a doorway, taller than the level of the styrofoam panels that make up the low ceiling.

She sneaks through the room and opens the door, finding that it opens to the outside, looking out into the little side yard of the house. Of course, she thinks, why had I never noticed this door before?

The morning air outside is cool on her skin, and she drops her slacks, squatting and taking a piss. She even smokes a cigarette. Even in the early morning, a few birds are already singing. The cul-de-sac in which the little house sits backs up to a parking lot with a little strip mall. A Sherwin Williams paint shop, a Taco Bell, a thrift store, a Shark's pool bar. Johanna walks through the backyard of the house, into the parking lot, and goes into the pool bar for a drink.

At the bar, she sits on a high chair and leans with her elbows on the bar top. There is no one else in the place, except for a bartender that has one eye that drifts to the side as she looks at Johanna.

I'm just about to close up, says the bartender, walking down to where Johanna is seated. You wanna beer?

Ya, says Johanna.

The space is open, with at least twenty pools tables standing around, quiet, unused, green; the soft felt of the those smooth planes now lying dark beneath the lightless Budweiser lamps that hang from chains above. In their bellies, the bowels of which are traced through with passages criss crossing from pocket to pocket, the colored spheres lie lined up behind a glass window, each one numbered and painted to correspond with their roles in the game.

My name's Gina, says the bartender, setting a beer down in front of Johanna. How's your night been?

I'm on break from work, says Johanna.

Night shift?

Something like that.

Where do you work?

The bartender wears a tank top and gym shorts, the front of which is stretched with her gut, double pouches of skin hanging almost to her knees.

I work at Lorna's, says Johanna.

They're kinda nutty over there, ain't they? says Gina.

Ya, nutty says Johanna, letting the cold beer slide bitterly across her tongue. But I'm making a killing this tax season.

Money ain't everything.

It's only for a little while. I'm saving up to go to Nashville.

Nashville?

Ya. I'm gonna be a country music singer.

Gina sets up the lights and the karaoke machine and, standing on a little wooden dance floor in the back of the bar, Johanna grips a microphone tightly with both hands and sings Dylan's Like a Rolling Stone as passionately as she can. When she finishes, Gina claps loudly for her.

What does your family think of you going to Nashville? she says, as Johanna climbs back onto her seat at the bar and takes a drink of her beer.

Opening the top three buttons of her blouse, Johanna peels back the flap to reveal a pale chest, in the left side of which a thin piece of skin has overgrown a hollow cavity.

You see this hole? she says, poking at the stretched flesh with her finger. I don't have a heart.

What is that? says Gina. You ain't got a heart? How'd that happen?

I was the seventh of twelve children, says Johanna, fastening the buttons on her blouse once more. My parents were part of a small church, a congregation that believed the end of days will come in our lifetimes. I managed to escape, but the price was that I had to leave my heart with my father. He still has it to this day.

Gina clucks her tongue. Ain't that somethin, she says. You shoot pool?

At a pool table beside the bar, Gina sets up a tight rack and breaks it herself, the fat on her arms shaking tremendously as she drives the cue through the bald cue ball, sending it flying down the table. The balls break apart and scatter, knocking into one another, rebounding off the bumpered sides, spinning and sliding in striped and solid spheres.

Don't you have any dreams, Gina? says Johanna, watching the orbiting spheres slow, collide, and come to rest on the green felt.

Sometimes surviving the day is dream enough, says Gina.

She strokes the cue ball into the red striped 2, which is nestled closely to the bumper and now rolls cleanly along its outer angle, until it falls into the corner pocket.

I think you oughtta be proud of where you're at, Johanna, she says. Coming as far as you have already. Nashville's a tough place to make it in. What if your daddy was right, and the end of days will come in our lifetime?

The end of my days is coming, says Johanna, taking up a cigarette that lies smoking in the ashtray. And when it comes, I at least wanna be doing what I want to do, not what my father wants me to, you know?

Gina knocks another stripe into the corner pocket, drawing the cue ball back towards the center of the table in a fantastic feat of pool hall physics.

I used to want to be a pool player, she says, circling the table like a bird of prey. A professional. I spent eight hours a day in run down joints just like this, wasting my life.

As Gina drives the cue that slides in her fingers, a peculiar thing happens. The solid shaft goes soft, plunging lightly into the cue ball, which now also goes soft, and rolls wobbly across the table like a flubber ellipsoid, colliding with other spheres that go soft and wobbly; some breaking open like hard boiled eggs, revealing a chewy yellow center; some even defying gravity altogether and rising and floating above the table.

Indeed, within Johanna's own chest, as she watches this miracle on the pool table take place, a new heart begins to grow, cell division, mitosis rapidly proceeding; veins, ventricles and valves growing around an electric muscle that begins to shiver and pulse.

Outside, in the early morning, a dull light has begun to suffuse the parking lot; the Taco Bell sign that stands dark, the dark windows of the strip mall, a dumpster from which garbage overflows and spills onto the gravel.

Johanna leaves the bar, and makes her way back through the backyard of the office and into the little neighborhood, where the bark of a dog echoes emptily. The doors of the office are locked and, as a train howls down its tracks just a block over, Johanna figures this is as good a time as any to go to Nashville.

A Journey, Suspended

In the depths of the darkest winter, when your soul is suffocating in clouds of steel wool and knife sharp winds, Lisa is rolling a tire down Jackson avenue towards Truman. The street is ice, but there is a dusting of snow that provides a little grip beneath Lisa's shoes and it blows and swirls in the wind as well.

The tire is heavy. It isn't just a tire, it is a rim, too. In fact it is a highly polished rim, about two feet in diameter with a low profile winter tread tire around it. It weighs about thirty pounds. Lisa tried to leverage the rim onto the seat of a bicycle and transport it that way, but the rig turned out to be unwieldy and prone to slips on the ice.

Jackson Avenue slopes downward towards Truman, and Lisa walks backward down the street, letting the tire roll down hill in front of her, or behind her, whichever way you want to look at it. She keeps it before her with little kicks from her shoes. She has her hands in her pockets. They ache inside the baggy fabric of her coat.

At the intersection of Jackson and Truman, Lisa turns her tire and rolls it east down the sidewalk. Past a used car dealership, where, behind a chain link fence encrusted with ice, cars sit like ice sculptures sculpted with an elegant hand.

Just beneath the layers of ice and snow can be seen the orange numbers on the windshields that say $1500.

Next to the car dealership is a little restaurant, the front windows of which are completely fogged over; but in the corner a little patch has been wiped clear and a face looks out, watching Lisa.

She keeps rolling her tire. The snow and ice has been piled in rippled layers around the curbs where the plows have cleared the streets. She works the tire awkwardly over the peaks and valleys, pushing it over the scalloped edges of ice and then keeping it upright as it falls down the other side.

Truman now begins its long descent to the highway, and Lisa takes the bridge over the railroad tracks; the rail yard, the industrial warehouses of lumber, a metal recycling plant. A few trailer homes sit on a bluff overlooking the morass. Their rusty skirts overhang the edge perilously, succumbing to age and erosion; as if the dishevelled structures were ready to join their aluminum brethren in the depths below.

Along the highway, the big grain silos rise like great ocean beasts; their long tentacles reaching out to the railroad tracks around them, ready to swallow up the grain into their bellies and then slumber their long winter sleep.

Lisa rests for awhile in the parking lot of a gas station, and as she does, the sun disappears. Whether it rose at all that day is up for debate, so obscure was its glow behind the sheet of steel wool that closed the sky. The street lights stand painted with snow, their light filtering down from glazed glass, giving the air an eerie glow.

The dark buildings crowd the sidewalk on which Lisa now rolls her tire, their empty doorways and blank windows glowering. Above one window, a light flickers statically and in the glass, two legs of a pig turn easily above a flame. The smell of flesh and spice that wafts out makes Lisa nauseous.

When she reaches the pawn shop, the brick building is dark. The iron bars on the windows cast menacing shadows onto the glass behind them. There are ruts in the snow where the bicycles, lawnmowers, and scooters once sat on the sidewalk; tracks in the ice mark where they have been dragged inside.

Lisa wraps her knuckles around the metal door handle and pulls. Nothing happens. She can't feel the cold metal in her palm. She can't tell if she is pulling or not. She watches her arm jerk and she thinks she is pulling but the door isn't moving. In her ears she can only hear the wind, only feel its pull on her frozen legs.

She kicks the door and feels nothing. She hits the iron bars with her hand as hard as she can but it is as if the world has suddenly withdrawn, as if she no longer has any effect on it. After hitting the bars for as long and as hard she can, she can see the purple, swollen knuckles on her right hand and she winces, anticipating the pain. But it never comes.

She runs down the street towards the yawning structure of a gothic church, the bell tower of which stands silent above the buildings around it. Following a series of stone stairways, Lisa comes into a deep alcove within the church, the belly of which howls with wind invading through broken windows. A few scarves of snow scuttle in the corners of the walls. In the side of the alcove is a heavy wooden door and she pushes it open and walks through the doorway.

She is stunned to find the inside full of light. Not only is it full of light, it is full of people, as well. The congregation is kneeling on the kneeboards before the pews as the bishop sings an incantation, the choir behind him echoing his words. The voices carry up into the vaulted ceiling, high above, where the wooden tresses fly out from the buttress and shape stained glass.

Lisa finds herself kneeling at a pew alongside the other penitents. Ahead, in what seems an incredible distance, the bishop stands above the altar dressed in elegant robes. The choir beside him, too, is dressed in robes, although theirs are hooded and made of a coarse gray material.

As she kneels and looks at the other people around her, she realizes she can feel the lip of the pew in her fingers. She can smell the piney scent of the wood. Her clothes are no longer frozen stiff, but instead hold in the heat of her body.

When the congregation rises from the kneeboards and sits in the pews, Lisa settles into the comfortable warmth and sleeps. As she sleeps, she dreams of being a girl in school. The teacher is writing something on the board and she is having trouble understanding it. All of the kids around her are copying the words onto their papers, but she can't read the words being written on the board.

She jerks quietly in her sleep, trying to raise her hand to get the teacher's attention in her dream. Around her, the snow piles in drifts along the pews, falling through the broken slats of the church roof. It begins to cover Lisa like a white blanket, until there is nothing left but a soft, white hump.

An Atavistic Recidivist

At the bus stand on Mulberry street, in the West Bottoms, Sammy shoves his fists into the pockets of his coat. He would smoke a cigarette if he had one, but he doesn't. The security guard stands next to him in a puffy coat that wraps his great bulk in a thick layer of insulation. It's just the two of them at the bus stand, a mildly awkward situation. They stamp their feet and blow hot breaths into the cold air.

Around them, the correctional facility sprawls its lengthy arms, the housing units extending back, row after row, and the chain link fences surrounding the yards. Behind them, men walk in two's, side by side, discussing the fate of their souls in a devil's world.

I think I'm going to walk, says Sammy, after a little while of standing at the bus stand.

Where are you going to?

I got some family in the city.

Where the chain link and barbed wire ends, a vaulted highway runs along a row of concrete pillars. The highway reaches the pinnacle of the bluffs, the top of which is lined with high rise condos that overlook the bottoms.

I can't wait any longer to leave this place, he says.

Sammy walks beneath the highway as the high concrete shakes with passing cars overhead. From the drains on each side, melting snow falls and echoes in small pools in the street. On the other side of the highway rise the dark brick warehouses, their faces stained with the faded lettering of the old businesses, the Kansas City seed and grain co., the hardware distributors, the produce traders, the furniture makers, the launderers; all rowed in tight streets like empty shells on a necklace.

Sammy turns into an alley among the warehouses, and walks along the loading docks in the back of the old buildings. He stops now and then to look through a blank window frame and see the detritus strewn along the floor, great piles of plaster and furniture organized in some catalog of abandonment and disrepair.

He comes to a wide corridor of railroad tracks, where a solemn procession of rail cars passes in slow motion. The cars pass slowly, one by one, through the switch station, displaying the regalia of graffiti that decorates their sides. When the train has disappeared, he crosses the tracks and follows a steep decline of rocks down to the river.

The water spreads its broad surface out before Sammy, running its quiet course through the earth, its deep channel stirring and shaping things to come. At the river's edge, he sheds his coat. It lies forsaken among the peaks of rocks that protrude through the snow. Then his shirt, and pants, and his shoes and socks, too.

He steps out into those mercurial waters and is immediately taken by the current, the icy river sinking its teeth deep into his chest. His lungs contract and refuse to release. Something keeps him afloat on those torrid waters, the face of which ripples and curls in fluctuating patterns, and Sammy becomes another dark blemish among the eddies and floating ice.

He passes beneath the old railroad bridge, the rusted iron of which stresses and groans with the weight of a fully loaded coal train. As his limbs begin to lose the shooting shocks of pain and go numb, Sammy feels something grip his foot and pull it downward.

For a moment, he slips beneath the water and then pops back up like a bobber on a fishing line. And then again, the grip and downward tug on his foot, only this time it doesn't let go. The membranes that encase his foot feel like suction cups and he is pulled deeper down, deeper into the opaque solution of mud and debris.

Sammy feels as if he is dragged downward to a tremendous depth, and then he finds that the suctioned membranes have engulfed him, and he is no longer in water, but inside the organ of some creature. The tissue is slick and warm, not unlike a womb, and it enfolds and supports every crevice and crease in his skin. The pressure across his body is constant but pleasant, a warmth that seems to feed and nourish him as if it were through the process of osmosis.

Inside this creature, the world in which Sammy once lived and struggled to find place and purpose dissolves. He wonders why he was so distraught, why he sought conflict with everyone around him; those unbearable waves of emotion and pain seeming now so insignificant and petty.

But for Sammy, even that state of bliss and calm is momentary, and he begins to feel the soft, slick tissue around him convulse. It tightens first around his foot and calf and then spasms around his thighs and groin and back. He is shoved forward, head first, and he fights to stay within the organ but the forces of contraction are too strong.

He is ejected back into a cold, opaque world and when he lifts his head and opens his eyes, he is once again above water, scrambling in a shallow pool that washes idly against the river bank. As he stands and begins to walk out of the water, he looks behind him and sees a pale shape withdrawing into the depths of the river, the last glimpses of a fish sweeping hugely and then disappearing.

A light snow is falling and as it begins to accumulate on Sammy's naked skin, he feels all the old habits and conflicts congealing in an inescapable atmosphere around him, gripping him in an ice cold embrace. He climbs up the embankment, through the bracken that grows up along the river, and he starts towards the downtown airport that now lies before him.

He makes the long journey around the airport, following the chain link fence, until he comes to a gate that leads to an aircraft hangar. Inside, there are two small aircraft, and they squat silently on their landing gear, their propellers muted and covered with protective foam padding. As Sammy threads between them, the bottoms of his feet pick up the fine black grit that lies on the cement floor, indeed lies over everything within the hangar; the benches littered with tools, shelves filled with lubricants, and machining drills and presses that stand lifeless along the walls.

In the corner of the hangar, there is a light on that bleeds through a glass window and Sammy walks into the little office where a man sits behind a desk. The man is leaned back in a chair with his boots off, his legs and feet propped up on a space heater that blows warm air onto his socks.

When the man sees Sammy standing naked before his desk, snow still clinging in his hair and on his shoulders, he stares with his mouth agape for a moment, as if what he is seeing is not real; as if a naked man emerging from the darkness is not in accordance with his reality. When Sammy doesn't move or speak, the man stands up and takes another set of coveralls that hang on a rack in the corner.

You need some clothes? he says, holding out the coveralls to Sammy.

Sammy takes them and puts them on and then sits down in a chair, his body now visibly convulsing. The man, too, is shaking as he fumbles awkwardly with the space heater, trying to arrange it so that it blows on Sammy.

Are you ok? he asks. Where'd you come from?

I came out of the river, says Sammy. A fish swallowed me up and spit me out.

The man leans on his desk, standing over Sammy as he takes off his glasses and presses his eyes deeply with his thumb and forefinger.

You say you swam the river to get over here?

Ya.

What for?

I left the re-entry center, across the river. I just stripped naked and jumped in. It took me like a train and then I felt a tug on my foot. And I went as deep as you can go and then washed up here, on the other side.

Do you need an ambulance?

No. I figure I'll just sit here and warm up for a minute.

From a shelf along the wall, the man takes a pot of coffee and pours some into a mug. It steams in his hand as he passes it to Sammy. Below the coffee machine is a small library of technical manuals, a few of which lie splayed out on the desk, their white pages torn and smudged with greasy fingerprints.

You a mechanic? says Sammy, taking the coffee and blowing on it.

Ya, says the man. You'll have to walk all the way around the airport to get back out to the bridge. You can't cut across the tarmac. I'd drive you but I got a plane coming soon I gotta take care of.

I always thought I'd make a good mechanic, says Sammy. I've never had anybody teach me, though. I know what gets them airplanes in the air. It's the shape of that wing, the pressure on the bottom. And nobody told me that, I just knew it. I just get tired, you know? Tired of working for other people and making other people rich.

The mechanic brings out an old pair of boots from a locker and sets them on the ground before him. The beige boots lean at precarious angles as if they would fall over but Sammy takes them and shoves his stiff toes down their open gullets. He takes the coffee down in what seems a few strong gulps and then, rising, he walks out of the office.

Outside, he follows the long line of hangars and buildings until he hears the high whine of a turbine engine spooling. Looking through the chain link fence, Sammy sees the sleek business jet where it sits on the tarmac, waiting to roll onto the runway. He watches as the ailerons dip and flex on the wing and the elevators swing up and down on the tail.

Sammy holds his spot at the fence as the aircraft moves away from him, gaining speed as it heads back towards the river. The nose pitches up and the tires come off the ground in that mysterious moment when flight takes place. The aircraft crosses the river, and, as the pilot turns the yoke, he thinks he sees a pale fish sculling just beneath the surface of the water, about the size of a small boat. The pilot rubs the window beside him to better see the river below, but when he looks back down, the shape is gone, and there is only the long, muddy flow of opaque water.

You and Whose Army?

At the catholic worker house on 12th and Benton, J. sits across a table from a stranger. The stranger is telling him about his job. About how he maintains a fleet of garbage trucks. About how it is just him and one other mechanic to keep forty trucks up and running. He likes his boss. Sometimes his boss will lend a hand in the garage. The drivers, though, are assholes.

He tells J. he doesn't have time for their attitude. Sometimes he has to work twelve hour days to get a truck running. Weekends too. He calls the drivers dumb motherfuckers. They overfill the trucks and bend the hydraulic jacks that operate the loaders. He hands J. his phone and shows him a picture of a bent hydraulic jack as proof. J. looks at the phone and hands it back to him.

Before the food is served, they all stand in a circle around the room and hold hands. J. holds his hand out to the man across the table but the man clinches a fist and they hold knuckles together instead. Someone leads them in a prayer and then they sit down and the food is served.

The man talks to J. as they eat. They eat beef stroganoff with a salad and orange slices. There is another man sitting at the table but he doesn't participate in the conversation aside from a few incoherent mumbles. The stranger tells J. about how he drinks four thermos' full of coffee everyday. He says this as he lifts his thermos to his lips and drinks. He says the coffee evens him out. That it helps him sleep. He talks about his kids. About how he's not going to do them like his own father did him and disappear. He says he is paying for them to go to a good school.

When J. is finished eating, he notices the stranger has hardly touched his food. A lady comes by the table and offers them pumpkin pie but J. declines. The quiet man at the table who mumbles takes two slices. J. helps gather dishes and wash them in the back kitchen. He runs into the stranger one last time and says goodbye.

Outside, it is a warm night and J.'s bare feet slap easily on the concrete sidewalk. He walks down 12th street heading eastward. The building he leaves is a business front that has been converted into a charity house. Across the street is a church. Most of the other businesses have long been closed. A gas station. A fast food chinese restaurant. A used car dealership. J. wears loose, flowing clothing and with every step the fabric wafts out a cloud of human stench that hangs in the air behind him. His hair is locked in a cake of filth around his head.

As he walks, it begins to rain lightly at first, and then it rains harder. J. doesn't alter his pace, to quicken or to slacken. He lets the rain soak through his clothes, wet his skin. He wipes the water from his face with his hand.

Beneath a bridge, J. snaps his fingers and a small flame appears in a barrel. He removes his layers of clothing and hangs them from a truss where it meets a concrete stanchion. In from the dark and the rain, a few faces appear around the fire. J. takes a few pieces of pie from his jacket and passes them around for them to eat. They nod and smile. The water falls from the gutters of the bridge onto the ground around them, and the flames leap and lick the edges of the barrel.

Tell us a story J., says a face around the fire.

J. clasps his fingers together and sets his chin on top of them. He tells them about a committee in city hall that discusses the state of the city. He tells them that the committee discusses who will suffer and who will profit. They divide the city into sections and discuss how to keep them separate; how to police each section, how to educate each section and how to tax each section. They discuss the jail and how much money to set aside to incarcerate the poor. They discuss the best ways to round up the poor and keep them out of the way of progress.

There are businessmen, council members, philanthropists, police chiefs and superintendents. One woman's name is Jennifer. She is proud to be included among the business men, the politicians. She has worked hard to earn the right to be there. She reads books titled Why It's OK to get an A Minus. She gets titanium thank you cards from the Harvard School of Business. She expanded Starbucks from two hundred stores to two thousand.

On her way back from city hall, Jennifer rides the streetcar on Main. She admires its smooth operation, the progress the city has made in making it a reality. In the dark window across from her, Jennifer can see herself sitting in her seat. The other seats around her are empty. A brown leather bag leans against her leg.

She feels the streetcar glide smoothly to a halt beneath her, and then she sees a goat suddenly get onto the car. Jennifer doesn't know what to do. She is frozen in shock as she watches the goat jump and run through the car, easily mounting the top of the seats and circling around her. Standing on its back hooves, the goat is as tall as a full grown person, and as the car begins to glide forward again, the goat rears back and then brings its horns into contact with the glass window. The glass is shattered and then the goat disappears through it, as fast as it had come in.

When J. finishes his story, the rain has stopped but there is still a slow trickle of water falling from the gutter of the bridge. The faces around the fire withdraw and disappear. The fire consumes itself and dies. J. dresses, his clothes still wet. He walks the city, humming something to himself. What, you couldn't say.

Somehow morning comes; a warm, sweet morning. J. is rummaging trash cans on Broadway. In front of a coffee shop, he finds half a cinnamon roll. The people in the windows watch him. One man steps out of the coffee shop and gives him a dollar. He moves along.

He finds shade in the park down the hill from the Kansas City Federal Reserve building. In a clearing beneath overarching honeysuckle trees, he finds a few others with shopping carts and sleeping bags. They talk and laugh. Some shout and scream. He follows a few others to a neighborhood where they strip copper from abandoned houses. They pack the scrap in a shopping cart and push it across the city to a scrap yard. With the cash, they eat at the McDonald's on Truman and then they go to a bible study in someone's house.

It is evening now, and they sit on benches set out around the edges of the room. In the middle is a projector from which bible verses are projected on the wall and a man stands and talks about the dichotomy of a religion of creation and a religion of empire. He is short and slight of frame. He is white and probably sixty three years old. He teaches theology at Seattle University. He is balding but his gray hair is feathered and slightly ruffled.

He expounds on his theory of the two religions. He shows a slide that separates the books of the old testament and the new testament into the two different categories. He talks about the prophets warning against the religion of empire. How kings only take and take and take. That the price of security is your sons, your daughters. That the Holy Roman Catholic Church ultimately embraced what Jesus himself rejected.

He turns off the projector and they clap. Then they discuss. One man talks about his time in the communist party. He says he thought the communists were the only ones that cared about the poor. He says he wasn't looking for God but he found her in the poor. In the interactions. Not in the bible.

It's undeniable when you sacrifice your wealth, he says.

He talks painfully slowly. He interrupts himself and asks himself why he is rambling on.

Anyway, he says, Jesus says the poor will always be with us. But he didn't say anything about the rich. The rich can go fuck themselves.

And the proverbial camel through the eye of the needle! says another man. It can't be done! One or two in a thousand, maybe! Throughout history, there have been a handful. But the rest are fucked!

There is a cat screaming in the room. A woman gets up and pours food in its bowl. They talk about Jerome. About how he consolidated power and made decisions. About how Constantine killed his wife. Locked her in a sauna. One woman talks about how she accidentally found herself on the very bridge where the fated battle took place. Another man says it's nine o'clock and time to wrap up. They stand and shuffle about.

J. finds a girl named Jessica and gives her a hug. She inhales his filth, holds back her gasps as she embraces him. After a while she grows immune to it. She buries her face in the folds of his clothes, in the fabric of which mushrooms seem to grow.

Are you ready? she says, looking up into his face. She has blonde hair. Her teeth protrude wildly from her face. She doesn't try to hide them.

Tonight? says J.

Yes!

They drive out of the city in Jessica's car. Three hours to Salina, Kansas, a town in the grass. The tall grass stands head height, and covers long stretches of oil pipelines buried in the earth. The headlights of the car shine out into the infinite night, swallowed by the darkness.

Suddenly there is construction equipment. Excavators. Trucks. Dozers. The doors are unlocked. J. and Jessica set coffee cans full of oil and gasoline in the seats of the construction equipment. They poke holes in the cans. Jessica lights a match. J. snaps his fingers. The fires blaze like angels in glory.

They move up the line, where the new oil pipeline is being laid. Jessica has a torch. She lights it and the glow flashes demonically as the flame burns through the metal, piercing the steel pipeline. They laugh like jackals.

On the ride back to Kansas City, they are quiet, and J. falls asleep in the passenger seat. The skyline of the city breaks the horizon just as the morning sun begins to rise, and J. doesn't wake up until they take the Benton exit off of I-70. Jessica smiles at him as he looks over at her.

What did you dream about? she says.

I dreamed about you, he says.

Loneliness

The City Market sits on the south bank of the Missouri river, overlooking the broad, flat waters. The water looks granite, hardly moving. Unless you get close, and then you feel its power. The current is electric, pulsing. Those who swim its width do so with the fear of death chilling their bones.

Deep within the buildings that surround the open air market is a monument to those powerful waters. A steamboat that once traversed the river has been dug up from a cornfield, and its contents now sit within a museum for the public to see. It had ran aground on a shoal in 1856. The boat's paddlewheel, intact and original, stands thirty feet in height in the front room of the museum. The room has high vaulted windows, through which the sun blesses the wheel with its light.

Michael stands looking up at the woven wood and metal of the paddle wheel. The great slats web out from its center, bound together with iron straps and rivets. As the huge wheel spins before Michael, its paddles drip with water from the chlorine scented pool below. Suddenly, over a loudspeaker, a woman's voice says, The 3:30 tour will be leaving in five minutes from the gift shop.

And then a long, melancholy steam whistle fills the museum. Michael follows a group of people down a wide, concrete ramp that descends deeper into the belly of the building; deeper, where the contents of the past surface like a resurrected dream. From a deep, deep hole they have been salvaged and set behind glass to be viewed by the masses.

Clothes, hardware, tools, dinnerware, cutlery, silverware, china, gunpowder, tobacco. As Michael walks along the glass display cases, he takes in the detail, the craftsmanship, the design and form; a lamp that burns whale oil, its glass reservoir elegantly blown and bound with gilt trim; an ink pen from the south of France, its silver tip engraved with flowers to the very point; yellow, blue, green and pink buttons and beads; even a bottle of perfume that still leaks a faint aroma.

Michael stops before a particularly stunning piece. Mounted in its own display, a sword rests on a slightly sloped bed of blue fabric. The curved blade is flawless, etched with a leafy pattern down to the hilt. The sword's handle is golden with a ribbed, silver finger grip, the guard of which is upswept to a floral finish.

Leaning closer to the case, Michael thinks he can just make out a pink hue staining the blade. Suddenly, an alarm sounds, and the tour guide approaches him. Michael steps back from the case.

Please don't lean over the display case, says the tour guide.

I was just wondering how you remove the corrosion from the ferrous metals, says Michael.

Extending her arm, the tour guide points over to a brightly lit area where a woman is sitting behind a counter.

The young lady in the lab would be happy to answer any questions you have about the restoration process of the recovered items.

Michael follows the direction of her finger to the laboratory, where a few people stand and watch a woman sitting behind a counter. She wears translucent latex gloves that are too big on her small hands. Before her on the counter is a black leather shoe, laced with a fragile thread that coils on the white countertop.

The freeze drying process takes several days, she says, wadding crinkling tissue paper into balls and stuffing them into the shoe. Once the process is complete, the leather is completely preserved and impervious to deterioration.

The people standing in front of her nod their heads in approval of her work. One man is fat and he shimmies as he pulls his pants up over his belly. Michael shifts his shoulder to step in front of them.

I was wondering how you remove the corrosion from the ferrous metals in the collection, he asks the woman.

In a metallic tray on the counter sits an orange block of nails. The nails are cemented together with mud and the individual shafts are hardly recognizable.

You see these nails? says the woman, taking the discolored block into her hand. The reason the mud around the nails has turned orange is that it has eaten into the metal of the nails and has absorbed the corrosion. So all we do is lightly work the nails loose from the mud with a small hammer and chisel and then coat them with a layer of preserving agent. That's why all the iron pieces you see in the museum are colored black.

From his coat, Michael takes a jar filled with brown liquid and holds it up. In the laboratory light, a gritty sediment can be seen suspended in its substrate.

This is a solvent I've been working on, says Michael. I developed it myself. It's completely biodegradable. It won't harm the environment, and it won't hurt the metal you are trying to clean. You can submerge any piece of metal in this solvent, no matter how corroded, and it will come out clean in forty eight hours.

Now the woman behind the counter and the people watching her, too, are looking at Michael's jar. The liquid trembles in the glass. Onto the wooden floor at Michael's feet, a warping star of light is refracted from the solvent.

That's really interesting, says the woman.

I was wondering if you would want to try it on your nails. I could sell it to you in bulk, wholesale. I know you have years of cleaning yet to do.

The woman behind the counter gathers her hair from around her neck and passes it over her shoulder, the loose gloves on her hands crinkling. The other people in the observation area begin to scatter, spreading out to the display of knives, hats, and flintlocks.

We have a very strict procedure we follow, says the woman. We work closely with the national institute of conservation to achieve the best results.

Ya, but you can just try it. I can leave this jar here and you can see for yourself. It won't hurt to just try it.

I'm sorry. I don't have the authority to make that decision, and the person who does isn't here. If you would like, you can get our official contact info from our website and send a message through those channels.

Michael returns the jar to the folds of his coat and follows the rest of the tour through the winding tunnels. They show a video about the excavation of the steam boat, how its exhumation came into being. Sitting alone in a dark room, Michael watches the screen flicker into life. Then a lonely violin begins to wail, and the grainy image of a man looking longingly into the distance appears. This is the story of a journey... says the video.

Michael sits back in his chair and sighs. He looks around the room to make sure no one else is there. There are only a few chairs with their empty backrests poking up into the light of the projector. The film stutters at points and the sound is slightly off.

When Michael exits the museum, and walks outside, he blinks and rubs his eyes in the evening light. He puts on his coat and then follows the sidewalk up through City Market, where the goods sit piled on tables on either side. The glass enclosures have been rolled down to guard against the cold, but inside, the stalls are filled with produce, as if there were no seasons in Kansas City. As if the earth, in its generous bounty, is not scant with its fruit in the depths of January.

For a moment, Michael stands and watches a man play the flute. He sits on a bucket between two vendor stalls. His fingers pad softly across the chromed keys, and the notes, too, mimicking his fingers, pad softly across the vendors' tables. The man doesn't look at Michael, but seems to look out of the corner of his eye towards the ground, with his flute pointed slightly downwards.

After he leaves the market, Michael follows fourth street down to where a bench sits before a railing on a little prom-ontory. The river now sits sunk in the glow of twilight. The only indication of movement on its granite surface is the slow passing of ice like clouds across the sky.

Michael watches the long back of a train slither along the river bank, and then shunt back through the West Bottoms. It winds through the old abandoned warehouses, where the cattle would come to be slaughtered and sold; where the migrants moving west would stop and gawk at the neverending rows of filthy livestock pens.

Immediately below him is a row of sheds whose roofs have caved in, exposing their rafters like an old skeleton. Their walls are now galleries for budding graffiti artists. The spray paint on the walls matches perfectly the purple colored sky, and Michael thinks it is the loneliest color he has ever seen.

Two Tangents on a Line

1.

Francis sits in a little cafe on 20th and Broadway. It might be a coffee shop. It might be someone's home. It is spacious. It sits in the corner of a building with big windows that make up two of the walls. Out the windows, Francis can see downtown, set in the glow of evening light. The building is on a rise and the skyline spreads out below.

How did Francis get here? How did he end up at a little table in the corner? He has no money. He can't buy coffee. He has none of the accoutrements that accompany coffee shop customers. In fact, there are no other customers in the room.

There is only one other person in the room. He is the owner of the cafe, and his name is David. But he's not really in the room. He is in a space that is sectioned off from the room. Within, he can be heard yelling. There is music playing in the room, so his words are muffled, but he is definitely yelling something. When he comes out, he is sitting in a chair that rolls across the tiled floor. The tiles are the color of adobe, long since faded and scuffed.

David has a book in his lap, an encyclopedia of ancient Mayan slingshots. He rolls over to Francis' table, and begins to talk about the book. He wears a bandana on his head, and flips through the pages as he talks. Francis isn't interested, but David talks anyway.

He talks about how the slingshot was sacred in Mayan culture. How it had a very exact, purposeful form. It was useful as a weapon, but also as an aesthetic piece of art, pleasing to the gods. The craftsmen who moulded the slingshots out of the sacred trees were held in high esteem. They were regarded not only as woodworkers but also as healers and in some cases prophets.

David pauses and looks up from his book at Francis.

What do you think about that?

I don't really know, says Francis.

Would you like to work here?

Francis looks around the room. There is an espresso machine on a counter, behind which sits a refrigerator and a gas oven with a stove top. The walls are covered in art. There is no blank space. There is a long, tall bookshelf. Some of the books have fallen and lie like suicides on the floor.

Doing what? asks Francis.

But David doesn't say.

When he leaves, Francis says he might show up in the morning for work. He probably won't. He walks south on Broadway, away from the cafe. It is a hot evening. He climbs the big hill up to midtown, and when he gets to thirty seventh street, he is sweating. He takes a right down to Valentine, where a big house sits on the corner. It is a meeting house for a local writer's group. Francis follows the sidewalk up to the big porch and climbs the steps up to the door.

It is a double door that is tricky to open. The thumb press on the handle sticks and it's not clear whether the door opens in or out. Francis struggles for a minute, the glass in the door rattling as the group inside turns and watches him. They are gathered in a circle in a large room and someone is reading something to which they are trying to listen. The door rattles louder and louder.

When the door finally opens, Francis huffs in and takes a chair just outside of the reading circle. Some of the members of the group scoot their chairs back so Francis can be included. There is a woman standing and singing. She slaps her hip to keep the beat. It's an old blues rhythm. She sings about a green eyed monster that roves the dell and kills women, Jealousy.

When it is Francis' turn to read, he says, I don't have anything to read, but I have a performance piece. Is that ok?

Sharon looks at him in surprise. She is the woman who was singing.

You can do anything you want here, she says. As long as you're real.

Francis stands and walks to a clear area in the room. The group's eyes follow him. He lies down on his back and puts his hands up in the air. Then he kicks his feet and begins to scream. He looks like a child having a fit. The group is not pleased. He stands up and returns to his seat.

Sharon looks at him and says, That was a deep well. You fell for two minutes.

How did you know? says Francis.

We're all falling down a well, says Sharon. And when we hit the bottom, we're dead.

When Francis leaves, it is dark outside, but still hot. He walks back down Broadway, towards downtown. He turns up Southwest Boulevard towards Main. Beneath the Charlotte street bridge, there is a group gathered around a fire. The fire burns in a barrel that has been cut down to a short height. There are only disembodied faces around the fire, as if limbs and torsos are not to be trusted. Francis joins them.

The faces pass a loaf of bread around the fire. And then a bag of lunch meat. And then a bottle. There is an old face. It hangs lower than the other faces. The old man's expressions are sincere. His eyes glow wildly. He talks about how he is hard of hearing. How his ears were deafened by gun blasts in the war. Which war, he doesn't say. Now, there is only ringing. So he watches faces. And he believes in the sincerity of the faces around this fire. He can read expressions.

He says the worst fascists won world war two. He says that all the sides were fascist, but that the worst side won. He talks about floating a peace flotilla to Cuba. Some of the other faces around the fire begin to grow impatient. They abuse him. They tell him he's a crazy old man. Finally, he tells them of his purpose to go to the border. To fight the injustices taking place there.

How are you gonna get to the border old man?

I have a truck.

Where the fuck did you get a truck?

I stole it.

You're gonna drive a stolen truck to the border?

Francis tells the old man he will go with him. They leave in the morning. The old man turns out to actually have a truck. It is a nineteen eighty one Chevy; the small body kind that were made in Mexico when they first started moving their manufacturing plants across the border.

Francis and the old man can hardly fit into the cab to-gether. It can't go over forty nine miles an hour with two people in it. It sounds like a hornet.

We're not going to make it to Texas, says Francis, shouting over the noise of the exhaust.

The old man doesn't hear. Or maybe he pretends not to hear. Noxious fumes enter the cab through the vents and they have to keep the windows down to clear out the smoke. After ten straight hours of driving, with only one stop at a gas station in Oklahoma, they make it to Texas. They make it to Dallas. In a hotel parking lot, they stop to sleep. Francis sleeps in the bed of the truck. The old man sleeps in the cab.

At eleven forty nine p.m., Francis is awakened by the flashlight of a policeman shining in his eyes. There is another policeman shining his flashlight into the cab of the truck.

Get out of the truck, says the policeman.

They tear the truck apart. It turns out to be a simple job as the truck is falling apart, anyway. Francis and the old man sit on the curb and watch. The old man tries to run. He doesn't get far. The other policeman tackles Francis as if he were running, too.

I'm not resisting! shouts Francis.

In jail, Francis is stripped of his shoelaces so as not to harm himself or anyone else. He is kept in a holding cell alone until he is processed into the general population. He doesn't see the old man. Francis has never been in jail before. It isn't at all how he imagined it. It is like a summer camp for fucked up people. They all sleep together in a long hallway. They have little cubicles that separate the beds. Francis isn't sure where the guards are. He just follows the routine with everyone else; to the chow hall, to the showers, to the rec hall.

He meets someone named Andrew. Andrew sneaks into his bed one night and jerks Francis off. They sit in the smoking area and smoke together. Andrew is small with glasses. He is the antithesis of a jailbird. He tells Francis about his foster family. His foster dad was named Jackson. Jackson was an army vet. He parachuted into Panama and broke his legs. He walked kind of funny.

When Francis gets a court date, they dismiss his charges. He doesn't know why. The judge seems distracted and doesn't make eye contact with anyone. If Francis could make a wager, he would wager that the judge was on drugs. He is in the courtroom for a grand total of five minutes and fifty three seconds and then he is outside, just like that. He is given back his shoelaces.

He hitchhikes down to the border. Down to El Paso. In the Texas wilderness, there is a tent city that houses migrant children. There is also an encampment of protesters opposed to the imprisonment of children. They eye Francis warily. They eye each other warily. The cops drive slowly around the protesters' encampment. They shine their lights into the tents at night. They blast heavy metal music towards them. They are police, FBI, border patrol, ICE, army and private contractors.

The protesters begin to fracture. They accuse one another of failure. Failure to act. Failure to have the courage to stop what is happening. Failure to stand up to a police state. When conditions are at their worst, something happens. There is a child in the desert. How it got there, no one knows. The police surround the child. So do the protesters. There is a standoff. The police demand that the protesters hand over the child.

The child is Mayan. She carries a slingshot. It is of an elegant design, and it fits her hand perfectly. She pulls back the gummy strands as if to fire. Whether or not there is a projectile in the web of the sling, no one can tell. The police, too, raise their weapons. The protesters begin to shout and scream. The bullet fire is dense. The bullets, in the air, are dense. Everyone falls. Except for the child. She lets the rock fly and it lands in the forehead of a policeman, laying him flat on his back.

The policeman feels as if he is falling down a well. A deep, deep well. He falls for longer than he can keep track of. It is dark. As he falls, he thinks of his wife. He thinks of the argument they had before he left for work that morning. The night before, he had wanted to see a movie. His wife didn't want to go. At first, she had said she didn't want to see the movie that he wanted to see. When he offered to see a different movie, she declined again. A resentment grew in his chest. She never had the energy for him. She was so dedicated to her job that she had nothing left to give him.

But he couldn't tell her that, because it felt childish to get upset over a movie. And so he had read his book, and she had read hers. They went to sleep without talking to one another. In the morning, he told her about his feelings. And now here he is, falling down a well.

He feels stupid. Stupid for getting angry over a movie. Stupid for standing in the place where there just happened to be a rock in front of his forehead. He knows this is probably the end. He had waited to have children and now he was probably going to regret it. There would be no pleasures of fatherhood. No losing sleep over a crying baby. No recognizing his own features in the soul of another person.

Was that the purpose? To leave behind a part of yourself in someone else? It must be, and he had failed to do it. The indelible mark he would leave on the earth would be the body print in the sand where he fell dead from the rock of a Mayan slingshot.

2.

The story of David and Goliath is narrated in the first book of Samuel, in the seventeenth chapter of the bible. It has been related countless times in countless churches across the United States. One such church is in Marble City, Oklahoma. It is called the First Pentecostal Church, and the structure itself is a double wide trailer that sits up on a series of cement blocks. The steepled roof is crowned with a cross.

Inside, Carl stands at the pulpit and reads from the bible. His crowd is not enthusiastic, but the entertainment in and around the little town is thin; even thinner on Sunday mornings. And Carl's wife's piano playing isn't bad. Her singing, though, is wretched. The group works together to drown her out when they are singing hymns.

When Carl finishes reading the passage of David and Goliath out loud, he takes off his glasses. Carl is short. He has hunched shoulders. In his retirement, he felt the call of God to minister to the people of Marble City. He looks out at his flock. They sit in metal chairs, sweating. There is a ceiling fan above that turns too slowly, as if the motor is burnt out. The blades droop downward as if they have melted in the heat.

Carl talks in a shaky voice. He talks about God being greater than any giant. How a simple faith in God can conquer any obstacle. What did Saul do? He hid. David had faith in God. He had the courage to face down the giant. Whatever obstacle you face in your life he says, addiction, anger, fear, sexual perversion, idolatry. God's love is greater.

He looks around the room for his granddaughter, Liza. She isn't there. She is out on A road, sitting on the old railroad bridge that crosses the river. They call it a river, but it's little more than a dried up creek bed. When the water is up, the kids will swim in the river and some of the older boys will jump off the railroad bridge.

From the bridge, Liza can see the highway that passes by the town. She lets her bare legs dangle off the bridge. She has just started shaving her legs. She hasn't told her grandparents. She likes to sit on the bridge and watch the cars go by on the highway. She imagines where they are going, where they came from. She imagines leaving with one of them, any of them, and escaping her hell hole.

She watches as an old blue truck takes the exit and drives down to the little gas station in town. The gas station, in fact, is the town. There are no other buildings in the town proper, aside from a few trailer homes. The old truck is unusually loud and seems to drive in fits of stops and starts.

Suddenly Liza leaps up and runs off the bridge. She runs down A road into town and when she gets to the gas station she is completely out of breath. But she stops and walks casually into the parking lot, trying not to breathe too hard. She gathers her hair behind her ears. The blue truck is parked in front of a gas pump and there is an old man standing behind it. He doesn't seem to notice her. She doesn't see anyone else in the truck.

As she enters the gas station, she glances at the counter and sees Francis standing there. He is counting change onto the counter top. The woman at the register sees Liza and says, Liza, if you don't leave my store right now I will drive out to your granddaddy's church and bring him back here and watch him whoop your ass. Do you understand me?

Francis turns around and looks at her. Liza is holding the door open and she looks at Francis and then she looks at the woman and leaves. Francis drops the rest of his change onto the countertop along with a few crumpled dollar bills. The woman takes them and counts them out and says, You want five dollars and thirty six cents worth of gas?

Ya says Francis.

Where are you going?

To the border.

What are you going there for?

I don't really know, says Francis.

Outside, Liza is enjoying the breeze passing through her hair. The old man has noticed her now and he watches her as he works the gas nozzle into the tank of the truck. Francis comes outside and walks past Liza. He doesn't seem to notice her. She walks closer, playing with the windshield squeegee that sits in the blue water. The woman sticks her head out the gas station door and says, Liza, go on!

But Liza hides behind the gas pump for a minute and then reappears. She begins to squeegee the windshield of the old truck.

It won't do any good, says the old man. I can't hardly see anyways.

Where are you from? Liza asks Francis. He sits in the passenger seat with the door open.

We came from Kansas City.

Kansas City?

Ya.

My aunt lives in Kansas City. My aunt Brenda. Do you know her?

Aunt Brenda?

Ya. She's got brown hair.

Ya. I've seen her.

You're a liar. My aunt Brenda lives in Chanute. It's my uncle Byron that lives in Kansas City.

Ya, but she came up to Kansas City for treatment. She was in the room next to mine at the methadone clinic.

Liza stops cleaning the windshield for a moment to look at Francis. For a second she looks concerned and then she laughs.

So you're one of those dope heads. I bet you're on your way to Mexico right now to get a load of dope and take it back to the city. We see it all the time here.

The old man takes the nozzle out of the truck and puts it back on the pump. He sits in the driver's seat and says, That won't get us to the border.

Liza sticks her head in the truck and says, I can get you some money if you need it.

Francis now looks her in the eyes.

How?

My granddaddy runs a church not far from here. I can sneak in and grab the collection plate.

The church is just a little ways down A road and Liza rides in the back of the truck. Her heart is pounding and she feels like she is flying through the air. When they get to the church, she jumps out and runs ahead of them.

You all stay out here while I sneak in, she says.

We're not stealing from a church, says Francis.

Francis and the old man walk into the side door of the trailer and find themselves at the back of the little congregation. There are probably ten or fifteen people in the room. Carl pauses his sermon and looks at them. The rest of the congregation turns around and does the same.

The old man lifts his hands and says, The real fascists won world war two. I lost my hearing in the war, but I can read faces. And the faces I see here are faces of peace. I'm on a journey. A journey of peace. I floated a peace flotilla to Cuba. To break the embargo. Now I'm on my way to the border. To fight the injustice there. You're a peace loving people. We just need a few dollars to get us there.

Carl points to the door from the pulpit and says, Get out.

Outside, a member of the congregation catches up to them.

You fellas going to the border? he says. It's a shame what they're doing down there.

He takes a ten dollar bill from his pocket and gives it to Francis.

Take that for the road, he says.

Liza is lying down flat in the back of the truck, and they take her back to the gas station. As the old man fills the truck up, Francis tells her to get out.

You said you knew my aunt Brenda! says Liza. Well my daddy was her brother and he died in a car crash and my mama doesn't want me!

We're not going to a place that's any better than here, says Francis.

Filled with gas, the truck seems to run better and Liza watches it slowly gain speed up the on ramp like an airplane trying to take flight. She kicks a few rocks in the parking lot and then sticks her arm in the gas station door and flips off the woman inside.

She goes back out to the bridge. Sitting down, she thinks about how church will be getting out. How her grandma will make tuna salad. How a few members of the congregation will join them. It's all unbearable. Looking down the highway, where the hot tarmac disappears into the distance, she thinks she can see the border. It is like a magnet pulling her down the mouth of a funnel, down into a deep, dark depression.

About the Author

Christopher Aslan Overfelt lives and works on the empty plains of Kansas. In the summertime he grows cucumbers and in the winters he takes attendance at the local high school.

www.ingramcontent.com/pod-product-compliance
Lightning Source LLC
Chambersburg PA
CBHW020730100426
42735CB00038B/1661